FOURTEENER LIST

Front Range	Elevation	Rank	Page
Longs Peak	14,255	15	6, 7
Mount Evans	14,264	14	8
Mount Bierstadt	14,060	38	9
Torreys Peak	14,267	11	10, 11
Grays Peak	14,270	9	10, 11
Pikes Peak	14,110	31	12

Tenmile Range	Elevation	Rank	Page
Quandary Peak	14,265	12	13

Mosquito Range	Elevation	Rank	Page
Mount Lincoln	14,286	8	15
Mount Bross	14,172	22	15
Mount Democrat	14,148	29	14
Mount Sherman	14,036	45	16

Sangre de Cristo Range	Elevation	Rank	Page
Humboldt Peak	14,064	37	18, 20, Cover
Kit Carson Mountain	14,165	23	19, Cover
Crestone Peak	14,294	7	18, 19, 20, Cover
Crestone Needle	14,197	18	18, 19, 20, Cover
Mount Lindsey	14,042	42	23
Ellingwood Point	14,042	42	22
Blanca Peak	14,345	4	4, 21, 22
Little Bear Peak	14,037	44	4, 21, 22

Culebra Range	Elevation	Rank	Page
Culebra Peak	14,047	41	17

Elk Mountains	Elevation	Rank	Page
Castle Peak	14,265	12	38
Pyramid Peak	14,018	47	39
North Maroon Peak	14,014	50	40, 41
Maroon Peak	14,156	25	40, 41
Capitol Peak	14,130	30	42, 45, 58, Cover
Snowmass Mountain	14,092	32	42, 43

Sawatch Range	Elevation	Rank	Page
Mount of the Holy Cross	14,005	52	2, 26
Mount Massive	14,421	2	1, 25
Mount Elbert	14,433	1	1, 24
La Plata Peak	14,336	5	28
Mount Oxford	14,153	27	30, 31
Mount Belford	14,197	18	30, 31
Missouri Mountain	14,067	36	30, 31
Huron Peak	14,005	52	3, 27
Mount Harvard	14,420	3	32
Mount Columbia	14,073	35	33
Mount Yale	14,196	21	35
Mount Princeton	14,197	18	34
Mount Antero	14,269	10	29
Mount Shavano	14,229	17	36, 37
Mount Tabeguache	14,155	26	36, 37

La Garita Mountains	Elevation	Rank	Page
San Luis Peak	14,014	50	46

San Juan Mountains	Elevation	Rank	Page
Uncompahgre Peak	14,309	6	47, 49
Wetterhorn Peak	14,015	49	53
Redcloud Peak	14,034	46	50
Sunshine Peak	14,001	54	50
Handies Peak	14,048	40	51

Sneffels Range	Elevation	Rank	Page
Mount Sneffels	14,150	28	44, 48

San Miguel Mountains	Elevation	Rank	Page
Wilson Peak	14,017	48	56, 57
Mount Wilson	14,246	16	56
El Diente Peak	14,159	24	59

Needle Mountains	Elevation	Rank	Page
Sunlight Peak	14,059	39	5, 55
Windom Peak	14,082	34	55
Mount Eolus	14,083	33	52, 54

FOURTEENERS
COLORADO'S HIGHEST

A Photo Journey

Roger Edrinn
Photographs, Text, and Map

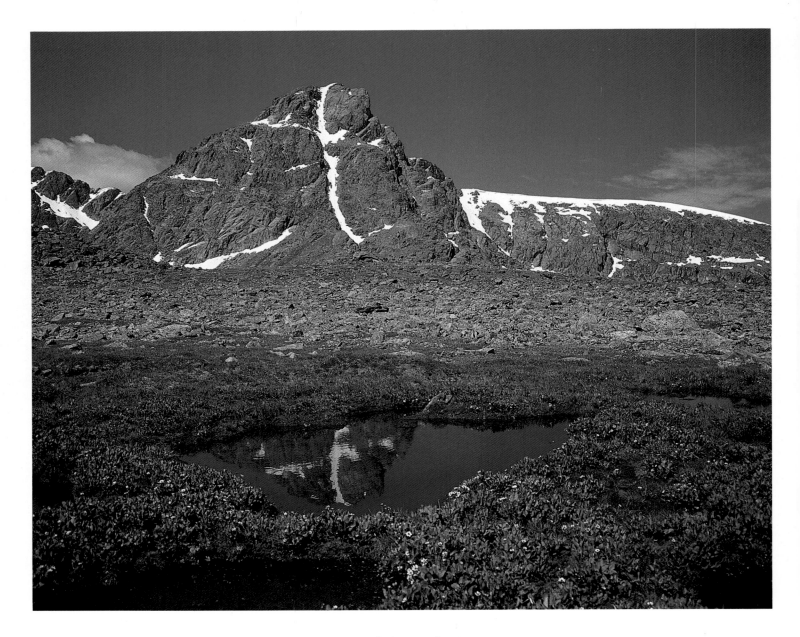

Mount of the Holy Cross

A collection of small pools encourage the water-loving marsh marigold
and reflect the namesake formation of Mount of the Holy Cross.

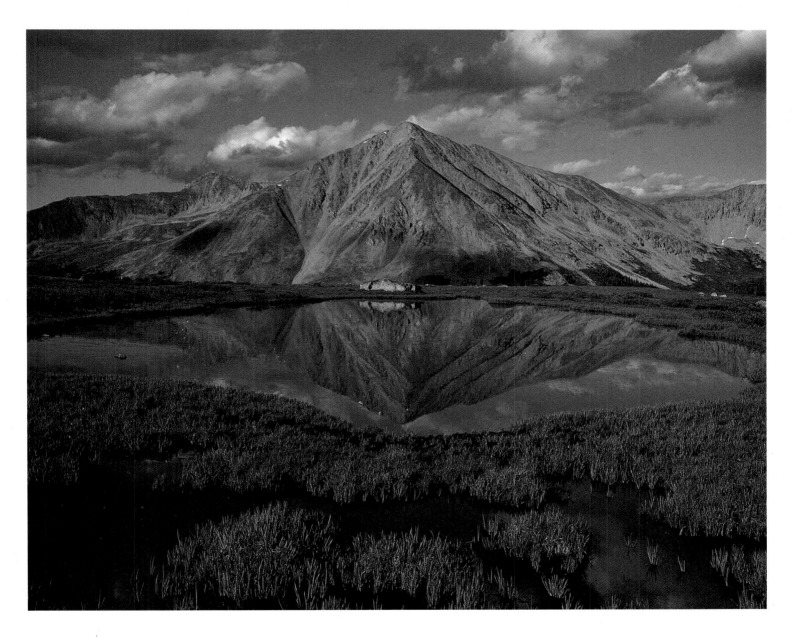

Huron Peak

A group of grassy tarns on Harrison Flat in the Collegiate Peaks
Wilderness Area mirror Huron Peak.

As I thought about my fourth Fourteener book, I contemplated what it should be, and perhaps more importantly what it should not be. My previous photo books had a chapter orientation based on mountain ranges. While a valid approach, it wastes valuable space in a sometime futile attempt to say something unique about each fourteener range.

FOREWORD

In this book I have retained the northeast to southwest flow of the fourteeners as in the three earlier efforts, but the slavish adherence to the dozen mountains ranges, which contain fourteeners, is abandoned. Instead, you will find more than sixty large photographs with captions that explain each photo, and add fun tidbits wherever possible.

Additionally, I wanted to honor Diente, whose enthusiasm for the mountains encouraged me to climb the fourteeners a second and third time. Those climbs provided many of these photographs. Enjoy!

Roger Edrinn

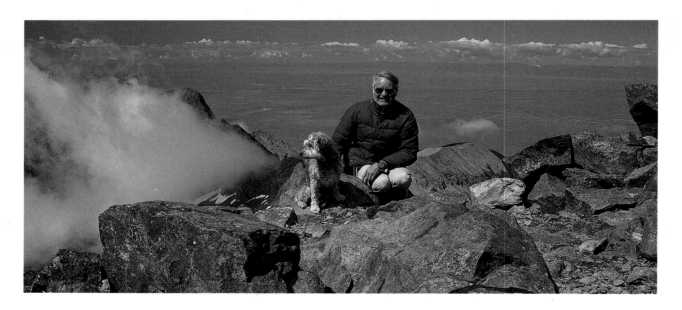

Above – Roger and Diente enjoy a sun-drenched summer morning on the summit of Blanca Peak, while the summit of Little Bear Peak is shrouded by a low lying cloud.
Front Cover – Capitol Peak is set ablaze at sunset.
Title Page – Colorado's highest summits, Mount Elbert and Mount Massive, rise above the foggy Arkansas River valley.

Page 5 – Diente stands next to the U.S.G.S. summit marker on Sunlight Peak, while in the background are the shadowed summits of Arrow and Vestal Peaks in the Grenadier Range.
Back Cover – The rising sun kisses the summits of the Crestone ridge showing: Humboldt Peak, Crestone Needle, Crestone Peak, Colony Baldy, and Kit Carson Mountain.

Published by: Above the Timber
2366 Wapiti Road
Fort Collins, CO 80525-3512
International Standard Book Numbers:
Soft Cover: 1-881059-85-5
Hard Cover: 1-881059-86-3

Photographs, text and map copyright:
© Roger Edrinn 1995, all rights reserved.
Design and layout by Roger Edrinn.
Printed in Korea by Sung In Printing America, Inc.

Diente was my constant companion and best friend for the better part of a dozen years. Life with this 30-pound bundle of muscle and fur was humorous, humbling, and a constant source of amazement. While he no doubt viewed me as the alpha male, this never made him too reverent and certainly not awestruck. Diente's life was driven by two lifelong quests: have fun, and inspect the world with his nose. These quests, combined with my mountain fever, created a high energy, mountain-loving, talus-taming, free-spirited, wonder dog.

Diente never struck me as a bright critter. I developed this attitude by his tendency as a pup to walk off cliffs and stand in front of moving cars. Just shy of his second birthday he stood in front of one such vehicle on a mountain road. That event earned him a compound fracture of his left hip and a permanent metal plate. As a result, his left leg was perhaps five degrees out from straight. Less than a month after the accident he jumped out of an open car window, risking further injury. Perhaps all this can be explained by the time, when he was less than two months old, he walked through a porch railing and fell six feet on his head.

What he lacked in brains he more than made up in energy and motor skills. He had catlike instincts to land on his feet from any contorted aerial maneuver. And as you will notice from some of the photos, he had no fear of heights. He also had no fear of lightning. This was especially surprising because he was terrified by gunfire and fireworks. Go figure!

In the course of Diente being the only dog to scale all of Colorado's Fourteeners, we had many excellent adventures and misadventures. One of the most dramatic occurred on the Maroon Bells. With both summits in the clouds, a climbing companion, Diente and I started early one morning from our camp high in Minnehaha Gulch. We made excellent time

DEDICATION

over the rock glacier and up the first steep gully of North Maroon Peak. Near the top of the gully, Diente did an aggressive leap up a short, steep pitch. His foothold was a piece of sharply angled maroon shale, and he slid off. I was directly below him, and the next thing I knew, he was in my arms. I immediately lifted him over my head and pushed on his backside until he got traction and he quickly dashed up

October 13, 1981 **Diente** July 12, 1993

the slope. The rest of the way was uneventful until I arrived breathless on the summit, whereupon a man from another party asked if that was my dog. Like a proud father, I said yes. He proceeded to lambaste me for bringing Diente on such a dangerous mountain. I responded, after catching my breath, that he was jealous that Diente and I had made it without ropes while he was "decked to the nines" with climbing gear. All the while Diente was asleep on a sunny rock.

After a short rest our climbing party thought the weather was breaking, so we proceeded toward Maroon Peak. The traverse went smoothly at first with the small ledges perfect for Diente's four-wheel-drive. Just

before the ridge low point, a ten- to fifteen-foot cliff presented itself. Since I was unwilling to let Diente jump that far, my companion positioned himself near the base, and I at the top and I grabbed the scruff of Diente's neck. I quickly swung Diente out over the cliff, he immediately went rigid, and I handed him down to an outstretched arm. Faster than you can read this, Diente was off and running as if nothing had happened. After the usual difficulties, the three of us reached Maroon Peak's summit.

After a two-hour traverse, the breaking weather had decidedly deteriorated and we headed down the southeast ridge. After descending about a thousand feet the rain started, and with it the sound of distant thunder. Within ten minutes the distant thunder became lighting strikes as close as two hundred yards with heavy hail. Before we got halfway to West Maroon Creek the ground was white with hail and we had seen Jesus. Oblivious to the danger, Diente just kept trucking. Was I ever proud!

Perhaps a more telling story of Diente's thought processes was when I was leading a party of nine up Mount Massive. On the way down the standard route, Diente followed his nose into the trees. Figuring he could catch us in a heartbeat, I paid little attention. After a half hour and no Diente, I became very worried. Apparently, when Diente emerged from the trees he could not find me, whereupon he started to retrace his steps. Three hours later we saw each other again at timberline, he going all the way to the summit and back, and I to the trailhead and back.

As I continue to travel throughout Colorado, I frequently reflect on our shared experiences and they always bring a smile to my face; a smile of remembrance for a friend lost, but never forgotten.

Roger

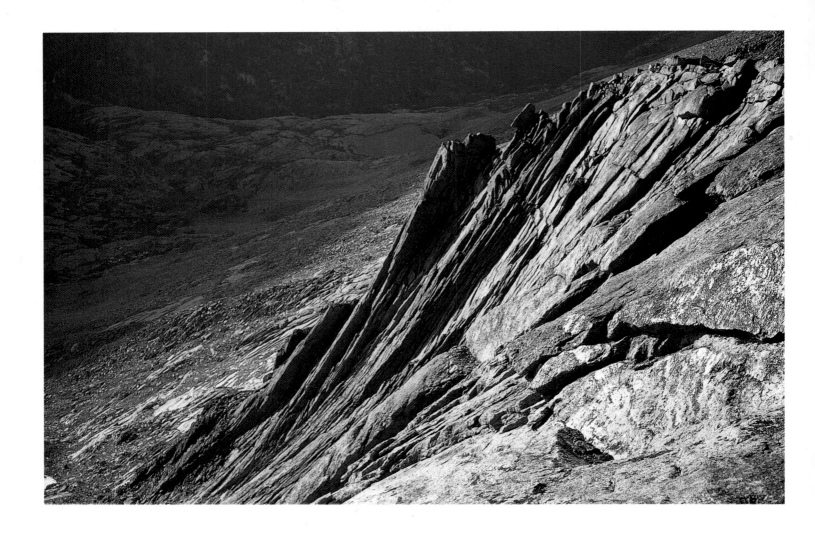

Longs Peak

This graceful rock form is the reason why the standard climbing route drops in elevation from The Keyhole to The Trough. Here, captured from the western edge of Longs immense summit, the fluted rock reflects a golden hue at sunset. Below in the shadow, a small lake shimmers high in Glacier Gorge.

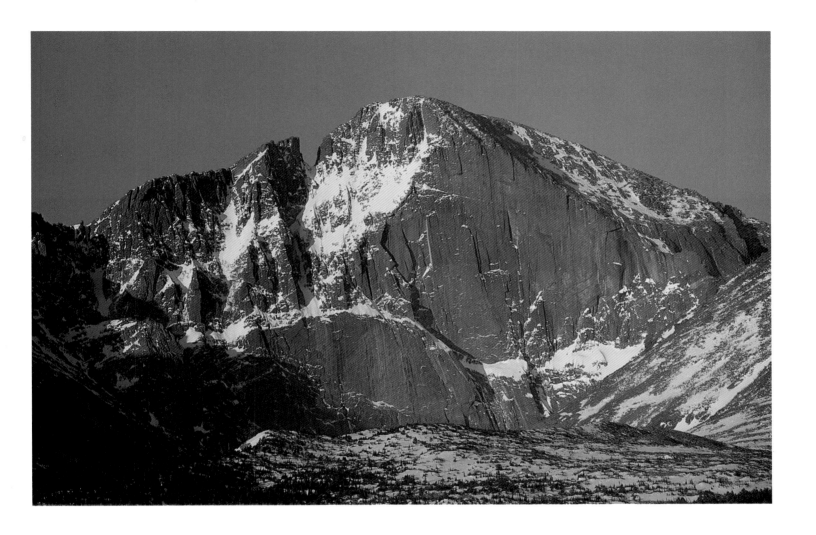

Longs Peak

The soft glow of sunrise illuminates the Diamond, the vertical 2000-foot northeast face of Longs Peak, 14,255 feet. This solid rock face is a favorite among technical rock climbers. For those looking for a less intimidating route, the trail branches to the right to almost completely encircle the summit.

Mount Evans

A rocky outcropping gathers sunset light north of Summit Lake. Although taken in mid-July, the lake still has an icy reminder of the long, cold winter at its elevation of 12,830 feet. Meanwhile, the last vestiges of a July thunderstorm break apart across the rugged summit of Mount Evans, 14,264 feet.

Mount Bierstadt

Late in fall the grasses turn golden around a rocky tarn and across the windswept upper slopes of Mount Bierstadt, 14,060 feet. This tarn is in the Mount Evans Wilderness Area, and is easily accessed from Guanella Pass. Easy, that is, if you don't mind wet feet traversing the willow bogs of Scott Gomer Creek.

Grays Peak • Torreys Peak

Not far from this spot a scenic railroad wound its way up the north slopes of McClellan Mountain. The railroad carried passengers from Denver to this overview of Grays and Torreys peaks. Grays Peak, 14,270 feet, and Torreys Peak, 14,267 feet, are among the easiest fourteeners to climb. This view shows the east face and the upper portions of Baker Gulch.

Torreys Peak • Grays Peak

High on a rocky ridge of Collier Mountain, the late evening sun casts a warm glow. Across the valley is Chihuahua Gulch, a favorite access route for climbing Grays and Torreys from the west. Grays Peak, 14,270 feet, and Torreys Peak, 14,267 feet, are respectively the two highest points on the Continental Divide in America.

Pikes Peak

This arch is at the base of the Siamese Twins formation in the Gardens of the Gods Park in Colorado Springs. Framed in the arch is Pikes Peak, 14,110 feet. No Colorado fourteener has more ways to its summit than the famous Pikes Peak. The Pike Peak Highway, the Pikes Peak Cog Railway, and the Barr Trail are respectively responsible for the most visitors to the summit.

Quandary Peak

Shrubby cinquefoil, commonly known as potentilla, is never so vivid as in its native high altitude habitat. Defined against the blue sky is the sweeping east slope of Quandary Peak, 14,265 feet. It is an easy climb in summer, particularly in pristine summer conditions such as this day.

Mount Democrat

One of the better fourteener hiking trails leads north of Mount Cameron to Mount Lincoln. Note several hikers coming from Mount Democrat, 14,148 feet. On the skyline, just left of Democrat's summit is the permanent snowfield of Mount Massive and further left is Mount Elbert, Colorado's highest.

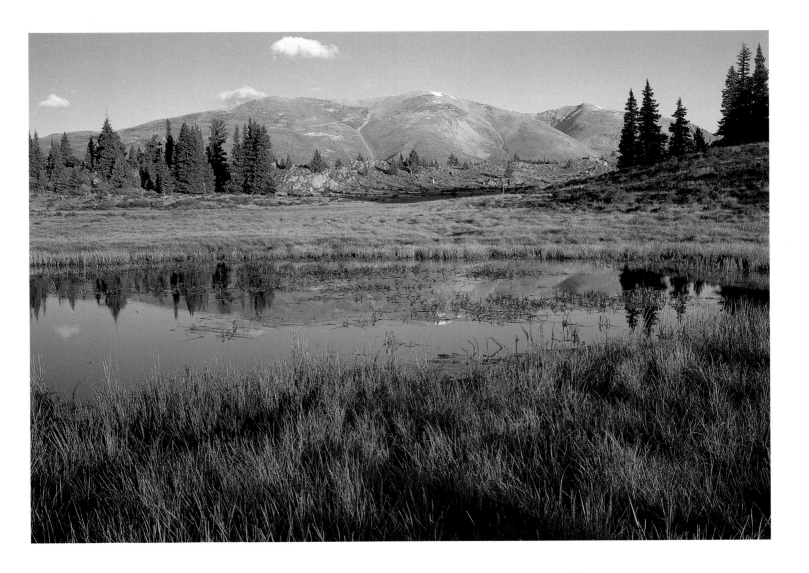

Mount Bross • Mount Lincoln

The rising sun casts long shadows across the waving grasses of an alpine tarn, while the higher slopes of Mount Bross, 14,172 feet, and Mount Lincoln, 14,286 feet, are fully illuminated. Bross and Lincoln had heavy mining activity and hence many roads and structures exist to this day. Careful inspection of this photo should reveal some roads, perhaps a tattered building as well.

Mount Sherman

Colorado's state flower, the blue columbine, grows in profusion on the south slopes of Mount Dyer. Across Iowa Gulch the abandoned Sherman Mine is visible at the base of Mount Sherman, 14,036 feet. The Sherman Mine ore body is actually several miles east and a multi-mile tunnel network carried the ore to this west side access.

Culebra Peak

Violet sky pilot add color to the high, rocky south slopes of Culebra Peak, 14,047 feet. The elevation here is almost 14,000 feet and still there is a profusion of wildflowers scattered in groups among the barren rocks. Culebra Peak is the highest summit in the Culebra Range, itself considered a subset of the Sangre de Cristo Range which stretches from Salida, Colorado to Sante Fe, New Mexico.

Humboldt Peak • Crestone Needle • Crestone Peak

The rugged Crestone group in the Sangre de Cristo Range contains the last fourteener to be officially climbed in Colorado. Crestone Needle, 14,197 feet, was first climbed July 24, 1916, by Albert R. Ellingwood and Eleanor Davis. Ellingwood's name graces many Colorado mountain features.

Kit Carson Mountain • Crestone Peak • Crestone Needle

The soft forms of America's highest sand dunes contrast with the rugged Crestone group. Kit Carson Mountain, 14,165 feet, Crestone Peak, 14,294 feet, and Crestone Needle, 14,197 feet, are the names man has given to these mountains. Also visible is a fourteen-thousand-foot sub-summit of Kit Carson, Challenger Point. Recently named to honor the memory of the space shuttle Challenger astronauts.

Crestone Needle • Crestone Peak

From the summit of Humboldt Peak, 14,064 feet, Diente intently peers into the abyss of North Colony Creek. His viewing technique was always the same—go to the very edge of a cliff and get his head as far over the edge as his meager counterweight would allow.

Little Bear Peak

The summit of Blanca Peak is Diente's perch for viewing the goings on below. Frequently his ears would "fly" from mountain updrafts, just like Dumbo. The forbidding Little Bear—Blanca ridge stretches between these two summits. Lake Como can be seen in the trees on the far right.

Ellingwood Point • Blanca Peak • Little Bear Peak

A grassy pool in the San Luis Valley reflects a western view of the Sierra Blanca at sunset. Identifiable are Twin Peaks, 13,580 feet; Ellingwood Point, 14,042 feet; Blanca Peak, 14,345 feet; and Little Bear Peak, 14,037 feet.

Mount Lindsey

The Sierra Blanca massif is mirrored on the surface of Mountain Home Reservoir. Blanca is Spanish for white and Sierra means mountains, so the Spanish name is very appropriate. Mount Lindsey, 14,042 feet, is the eastern white mountain in this group. The summits of Little Bear and Blanca are hidden in this picturesque wave cloud.

Mount Elbert

Early morning fog obscures the Arkansas River valley, while on the opposite side, Colorado's highest mountain stands serene. Mount Elbert, 14,433 feet, is most frequently climbed by either of the two ridges on either side of the prominent center cirque. The left ridge is accessed via CO 82, whereas the right ridge uses the Halfmoon Creek Road.

Mount Massive

This north-south string of multiple fourteen-thousand-foot points are what gives Mount Massive, 14,421 feet, its name. This view is typical of what one sees from the Leadville area. When viewed from the south near Granite, the mountain takes on a much more humble persona.

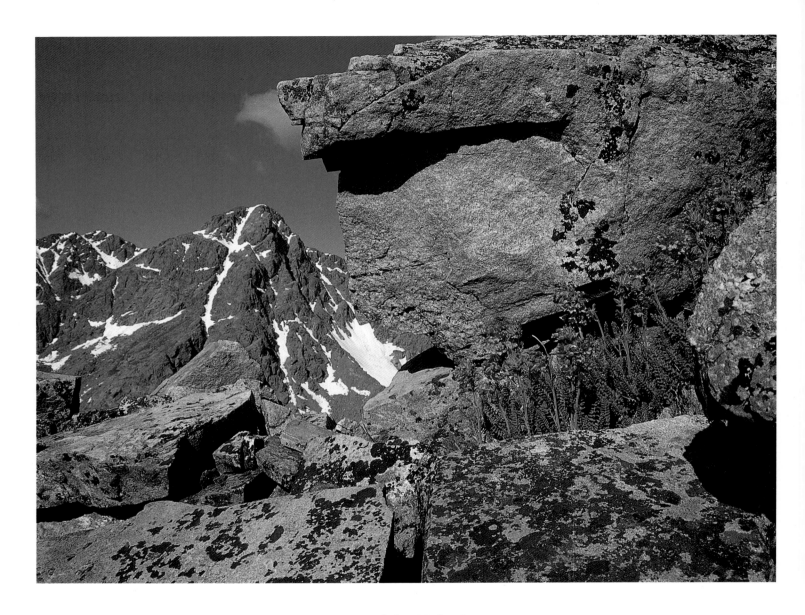

Mount of the Holy Cross

The high, rocky ridges of Notch Mountain create a sun-trap to nurture a small clutch of sky pilot. Mount of the Holy Cross, 14,005 feet, rises across the valley of East Cross Creek.

Huron Peak

A high-altitude summer morning provides a view up the Lake Fork of Clear Creek. Visible are Huron Peak, 14,005 feet, Browns Peak, 13,523 feet, and Middle Mountain, 13,060 feet. Just out of view, further up the Lake Fork is Cloyses Lake.

La Plata Peak

A stationary cloud reflects the last rays of light onto the snow-draped summit of La Plata Peak, 14,336 feet. Much of the La Plata climbing route is in view, particularly that section from timberline to the summit.

Mount Antero

The upper bowl of Baldwin Gulch, with one of its small lakes, is off to the left, while Mount Antero, 14,269 feet, basks in the reflected glow of a summer sunset. Hikers most frequently use the road, visible on the west side of Antero, and finish along the south ridge. The south side of Mount Princeton can be seen on the left skyline.

Mount Oxford • Mount Belford • Missouri Mountain

A collection of stacked stones and weathered boards is all that remains of a structure that was once part of the Columbine Mine. Across Clear Creek, three east–west fourteeners gather the last rays of a summer sunset.

Mount Oxford • Mount Belford • Missouri Mountain

About a mile further west, compared to the previous photo, the same three fourteeners bask in the sunset of another day. Mount Oxford, 14,153 feet, Mount Belford, 14,197 feet, and Missouri Mountain, 14,067 feet, are most commonly climbed from Missouri Gulch, partially obscured by the foreground rocks.

Mount Harvard

Just north of Browns Pass on the west side of the Continental Divide, the view to the northeast reveals Mount Harvard, which is on the east side of the divide. The divide is the low jagged ridge below and right of the summit of Mount Harvard, 14,420 feet. Just across the divide is Horn Fork Basin, the most popular climbing approach for Harvard and Columbia.

Mount Columbia

The waning days of summer see an early snowfall and the green willows take on a subtle golden hue. Reflected in this Frenchman Creek beaver pond is the north face of Mount Columbia, 14,073 feet. The rugged ridge on the right skyline connects to Mount Harvard and is the reason most climbers descend to this gentle valley. This part of the Frenchman Creek valley is in the Collegiate Peaks Wilderness Area.

Mount Princeton

The brilliant winter moon sets in the morning sky while the rising sun casts a warm alpenglow over the frigid surface of Mount Princeton, 14,197 feet. Most hikers follow a road below the left summit and then crossover to the main basin at timberline. From timberline an old miners trail continues in a long arc around the basin to the summit.

Mount Yale

Strong winds tear clouds of frozen snow off the summit ridges of the
Collegiate Peaks. Here Mount Yale, 14,196 feet, is awakened from a
winter sleep by the soft pink blush of sunrise.

Mount Shavano • Mount Tabeguache

A carpet of bistort on the flats west of Mount White provide a gentle foreground for Tabeguache's rugged north face. Mount Shavano and Mount Tabeguache are seldom climbed from the north owing to the difficult access. This in spite of the fact that the actual climbs are easier from this side.

Mount Tabeguache • Mount Shavano

A midsummer sunset peeks under the cloud deck to highlight the summits of Mount Tabeguache, 14,155 feet and Mount Shavano, 14,229 feet. Jennings Creek, the most popular climbing access, is visible above the shadowed ridge on the left.

Castle Peak

A snow- and flower-fringed alpine pond calms briefly to reflect the rugged summit ridge of Castle Peak, 14,265 feet. At the far right is Montezuma Basin and above its ridge is the crest of Cathedral Peak.

Pyramid Peak

A field of marsh marigolds high in Minnehaha Gulch soaks up the intense alpine sunshine, while across the valley of West Maroon Creek is Pyramid Peak, 14,018 feet, one of Colorado's steepest summits.

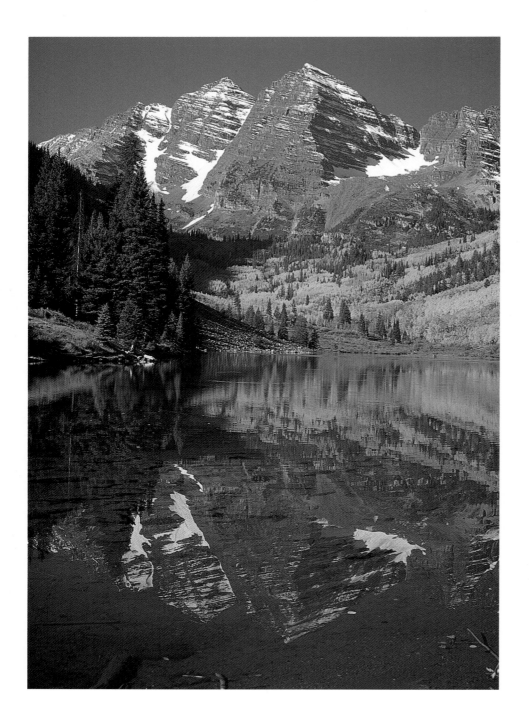

Maroon Bells

Perhaps the most photographed mountains in America, the popular Maroon Bells recreation area is closed to private automobiles most of the summer. A public bus is available in downtown Aspen for daytime sightseeing. These two photos of the Maroon Bells were taken less than two weeks apart. The completely different look is a testament to the variability of Colorado's mountain weather. Both photos are available as posters.

Maroon Bells

While popularly called the Maroon Bells they also go by Maroon Peak and North Maroon Peak. Both are difficult climbs owing to the complicated routes and the maroon formation shale, which is often slippery and always brittle. This perspective causes North Maroon Peak, 14,014 feet, on the right to appear higher than Maroon Peak, 14,156 feet.

Snowmass Mountain • Capitol Peak

The mile-wide, snow-covered east face of Snowmass is the source of its descriptive name. Here seen from Buckskin Pass, 12,462 feet, Snowmass Mountain is commonly climbed via this snowfield. The route takes you to the saddle between Hagerman Peak, 13,841 feet and Snowmass Mountain, 14,092 feet, then it follows the connecting ridge to the summit. Visible to the right is Capitol Peak, 14,130 feet.

Snowmass Mountain

The Pierre Lakes are among the highest and most desolate in Colorado. Seen here from a connecting ridge between Capitol and Clark Peaks, the lakes display their rugged beauty. Snowmass Mountain rises from the south end of the basin and on the far left the Maroon Bells are visible.

Mount Sneffels

The East Dallas Creek drainage is full of gorgeous groves of golden aspen and red oak. These colors play against the rugged summits of the Sneffels Range. Its highest summit and only fourteener is Mount Sneffels, 14,150 feet.

Capitol Peak

Capitol Creek flows north from its namesake through golden groves of quaking aspen and occasional groups of red oak. At the end of the valley, Mount Daly, 13,100 feet and Capitol Peak, 14,130 feet, dominate the azure late-afternoon skyline.

San Luis Peak

Lemon- and red-orange-colored paintbrush mingle in a grove of timberline willows on the Continental Divide. Across the divide the soft volcanic form of San Luis Peak, 14,014 feet, merges with late-afternoon clouds.

Uncompahgre Peak

High on the south ridge of Wetterhorn Peak, Indian paintbrush enjoy summer. The elevation here is over 13,000 feet, a testament to the hardiness of these flowers. Dominating the skyline, as it so often does in the San Juans, is Uncompahgre Peak, 14,309 feet.

Mount Sneffels

The rising winter sun creates jewel-like facets on the eastern ridges of the Sneffels Range. Most climbers use picturesque Yankee Boy Basin southeast of Sneffels to attain its summit.

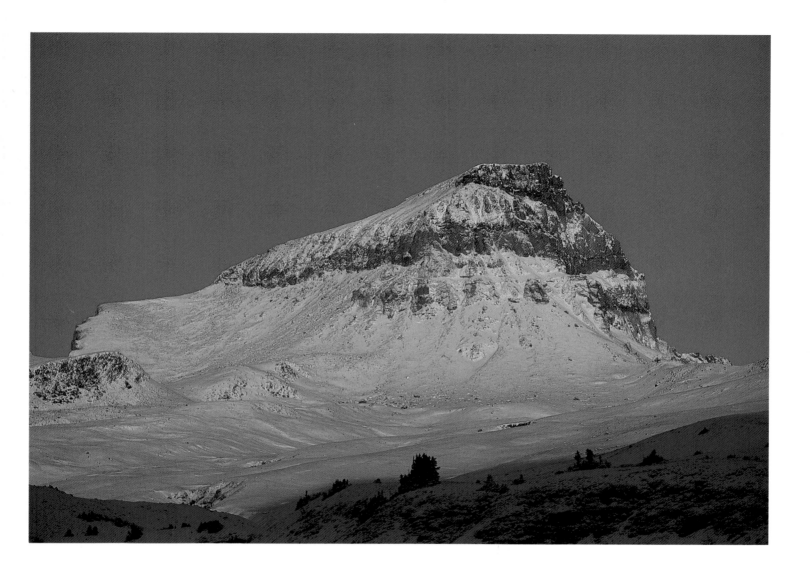

Uncompahgre Peak

A fresh overnight snowfall coupled with the just rising sun paints a soft glow on the east face of Uncompahgre Peak. The climbing route largely follows the left skyline ridge and, except for the cliff zone midway up, its quite easy.

Redcloud Peak • Sunshine Peak

The setting sun dances through the thin clouds in a show of Mother Nature's painting skills. Redcloud Peak, 14,034 feet, and Sunshine Peak, 14,001 feet, represent large piles of steep gravel to most climbers. The status of a day's weather is often the most memorable part of climbing these twin summits.

Handies Peak

Another gorgeous, albeit subtle, San Juan sunset. Here Handies is reflected in a large, grassy pond near Cinnamon Pass. Handies Peak, 14,048 feet, is easily climbed via either American Basin or Grizzly Gulch.

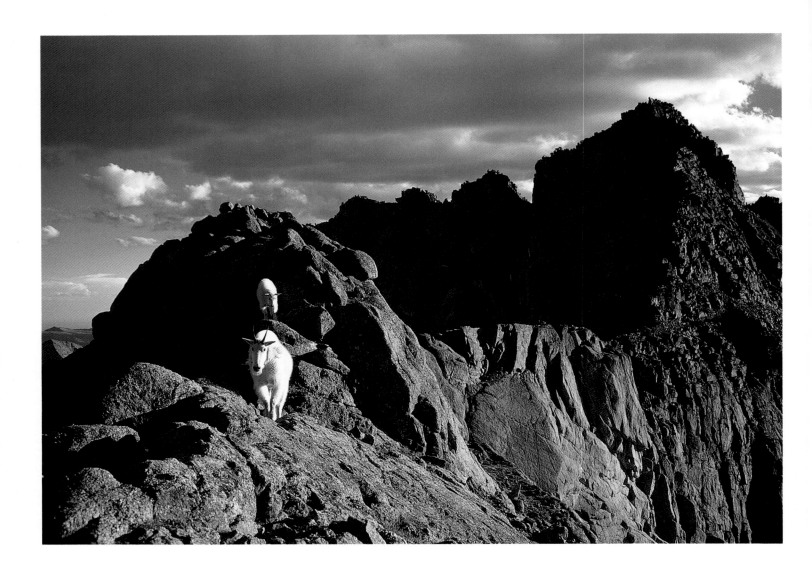

Mount Eolus

A mountain goat nanny and her kid cruise across the "Sidewalk in the Sky" to check out the visitors invading their high domain. Diente and I had just descended from the summit of Eolus when the goats appeared on the ridge. Mount Eolus, 14,083 feet, is the highest peak in the 492,418 acre Weminuche Wilderness Area, Colorado's largest.

Wetterhorn Peak

Perhaps the most common critter a climber will encounter, the yellow-bellied marmot can be seen everywhere in Colorado's mountains. Their sharp, shrill whistle accounts for another of their names, whistle pig. This one watches from a rock outcropping as I ascend Wetterhorn Peak, 14,015 feet.

Mount Eolus

It's late June and the twin lakes of upper Chicago Basin are still frozen. The sunlit summits of Mount Eolus, 14,083 feet and North Eolus, 14,039 feet, contrast with the shadowed Pigeon Peak, 13,972 feet. Surprisingly, Pigeon is the most dramatic of the Needle Mountains, this owing to its loner status to the west, and its 5,000-foot relief above the Animas River.

Sunlight Peak • Windom Peak

Across the twin lakes from Eolus and rising to an almost identical height are Sunlight Peak, 14,059 feet and Windom Peak, 14,082 feet. All three are considered difficult climbs, each with a unique set of problems. Climbers can be thankful that Sunlight is higher than Sunlight Spire, a thin rock column, just under 14,000 feet on the Sunlight—Windom connecting ridge.

Mount Wilson • Wilson Peak

A San Miguel panorama that starts at Lizard Head and sweeps to Wilson Peak, with a herd of two dozen elk in the clearing between the foreground trees. The mountain panorama consists of Lizard Head, 13,113 feet; Mount Wilson, 14,246 feet; Gladstone Peak, 13,913 feet; Sunshine Mountain, 12,930 feet; and Wilson Peak, 14,017 feet.

Wilson Peak

On the same high point where the Silver Pick rock bunkhouse sits, this group of magenta paintbrush add foreground interest to the west side of Wilson Peak. The far right saddle is Navajo Pass, part of the circle route used to access the final pitch on the east side of Wilson Peak.

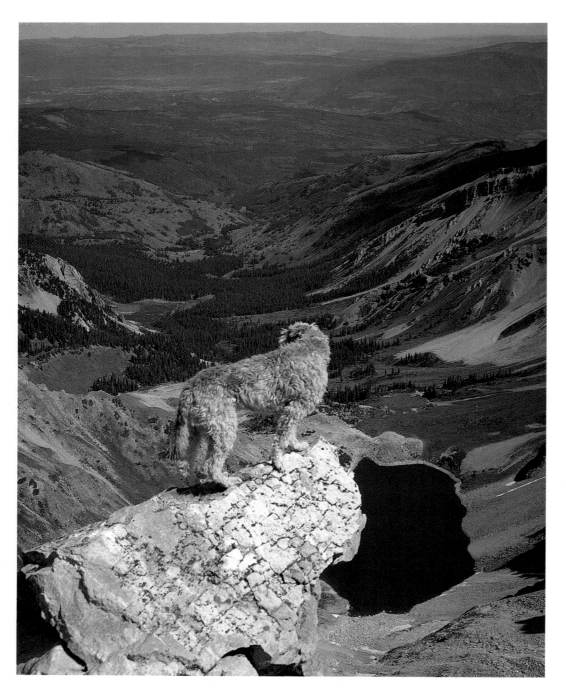

Capitol Peak

This thin piece of rock is actually more exposed that it looks. It juts out over the steepest section of the summit of Capitol and the first bounce is probably at least 100 feet onto an eighty degree slope. Look at the cover photo to get a sense of the "get-off" from this spot. Why Diente had to go out there is beyond me. Perhaps he wanted a better view of Capitol Lake, over 2000 feet below.

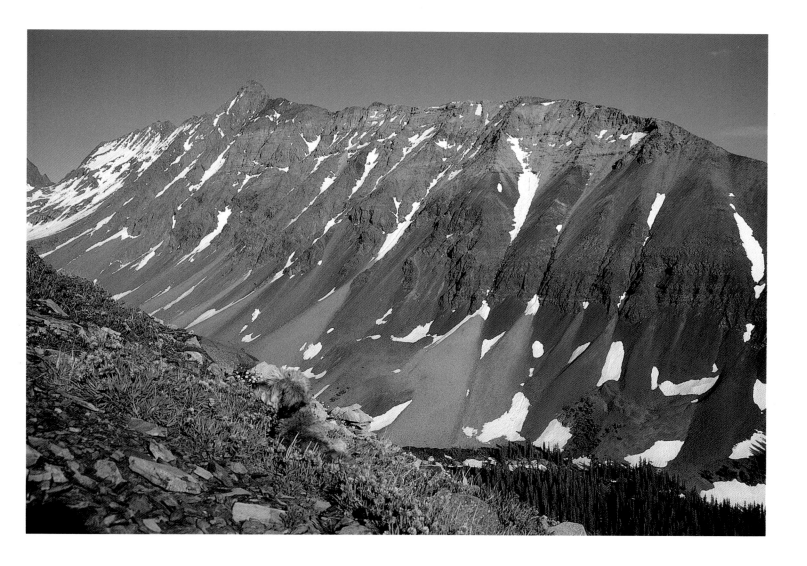

El Diente Peak

Occasionally, my photo assistant would nonchalantly lay down in my foreground. On most of these events I would gently shoo him away. Fortunately on this occasion I fired the shutter. If you have wondered what Diente's name means and thought there might be a connection to El Diente Peak, you're right. Both are Spanish for tooth and both were well named. El Diente Peak, 14,159 feet, has a distinct tooth profile opposite this Navajo Basin perspective.

FOURTEENERS
COLORADO'S HIGHEST

Longs

Glenwood Springs

Torreys
Evans
Grays
Bierstadt

Holy Cross

Quandary

Bross
Lincoln
Democrat

Massive
Elbert
Sherman

Capitol
Snowmass

Missouri
Belford
Oxford

N Maroon
Maroon
La Plata
Pyramid
Castle
Huron

Grand Junction

Pikes

Harvard
Columbia
Yale
Princeton
Antero
Tabeguache
Shavano

Gunnison

Salida

Colorado Springs

Montrose

Pueblo

Uncompahgre

Wetterhorn
Redcloud

San Luis

Kit Carson
Crestone
Crestone Needle

Humboldt

Sneffels

Wilson Pk
El Diente

Handies
Sunshine

Creede

Mt Wilson

Sunlight
Windom

Ellingwood
Little Bear

Lindsey

Eolus

Blanca

Cortez

Monte Vista

Alamosa

Durango

Culebra

Denver

FOURTEENER LOG

Front Range

Longs Peak _____

Mount Evans _____

Mount Bierstadt _____

Torreys Peak _____

Grays Peak _____

Pikes Peak _____

Tenmile Range

Quandary Peak _____

Mosquito Range

Mount Lincoln _____

Mount Bross _____

Mount Democrat _____

Mount Sherman _____

Sangre de Cristo Range

Humboldt Peak _____

Kit Carson Mountain _____

Crestone Peak _____

Crestone Needle _____

Mount Lindsey _____

Ellingwood Point _____

Blanca Peak _____

Little Bear Peak _____

Culebra Range

Culebra Peak _____

Sawatch Range

Mount of the

Holy Cross _____

Mount Massive _____

Mount Elbert _____

La Plata Peak _____

Mount Oxford _____

Mount Belford _____

Missouri Mountain _____

Huron Peak _____

Mount Harvard _____

Mount Columbia _____

Mount Yale _____

Mount Princeton _____

Mount Antero _____

Mount Shavano _____

Mount Tabeguache _____

Elk Mountains

Castle Peak _____

Pyramid Peak _____

North Maroon Peak _____

Maroon Peak _____

Capitol Peak _____

Snowmass Mountain _____

San Juans

La Garita Mountains

San Luis Peak _____

San Juan Mountains

Uncompahgre Peak _____

Wetterhorn Peak _____

Redcloud Peak _____

Sunshine Peak _____

Handies Peak _____

Sneffels Range

Mount Sneffels _____

San Miguel Mountains

Wilson Peak _____

Mount Wilson _____

El Diente Peak _____

Needle Mountains

Sunlight Peak _____

Windom Peak _____

Mount Eolus _____